# READ A POEM, WRITE A POEM

## AN ANTHOLOGY FOR 7-14 YEAR OLDS

Simon Ireland

# READ A POEM, WRITE A POEM

## AN ANTHOLOGY FOR 7-14 YEAR OLDS

**MEREO**
Cirencester

## Mereo Books

1A The Wool Market Dyer Street Cirencester Gloucestershire GL7 2PR
An imprint of Memoirs Publishing www.mereobooks.com

Read a poem, write a poem: 978-1-86151-697-8

First published in Great Britain in 2016
by Mereo Books, an imprint of Memoirs Publishing

Copyright ©2016

The address for Memoirs Publishing Group Limited can be found at
www.memoirspublishing.com

The Memoirs Publishing Group Ltd Reg. No. 7834348

The Memoirs Publishing Group supports both The Forest Stewardship Council® (FSC®) and the PEFC® leading international forest-certification organisations. Our books carrying both the FSC label and the PEFC® and are printed on FSC®-certified paper. FSC® is the only forest-certification scheme supported by the leading environmental organisations including Greenpeace. Our paper procurement policy can be found at www.memoirspublishing.com/environment

Typeset in 11/17pt Century Schoolbook
by Wiltshire Associates Publisher Services Ltd. Printed and bound in Great Britain by Printondemand-Worldwide, Peterborough PE2 6XD

# SCHOOLDAYS

# Flight of fancy

At the start of the year
I fashioned my ambitions
Into that paper shape
Familiar to so many schoolboys.

The question was, however,
Whether it would take flight,
Fuelled by hopes and dreams,
Its sharp white prow
Cleaving the cold January air,
Or whether it would sink
Unerringly to earth,
Weighed down by resolutions,
Its crumpled fuselage
A crash course in reality.

As I stretched my arm back,
Prepared to throw
Not just caution to the winds,
I somehow knew the answer already.

# Tree in the playground

I watch, as I have always watched,
The uniformed children swirl around
Like specks of blue confetti.
Each pupil knows this furrowed face,
These arms that keep the rain away.
My roots, meanwhile, soak up the laughter
That sustains me week on week
Then spread out beneath the feet that dance
And the skipping ropes that whirl and fizz.

But the summer months are lonely
For no one seeks sanctuary in my shade
And I wonder if they ever stop to think of me,
Those whose simple joys I've shared.

# The great debate

I set my friends a challenge,
To choose their favourite sport,
And convince me of its merits
On table, pitch or court.

'I like cricket best,' said one,
'It's a game of all-round skill,
It's embedded in our culture
And we hold the Ashes still!'

I played a dead bat to his logic
And let the next one take his turn,
He'd far rather hold the FA cup
Than a tarnished little urn!

'Soccer's the game for me,' he said,
For who hasn't kicked a ball
Or put jumpers down to mark a goal
By garden, park or wall?

I buy the kit that my team wear,
I thrill to every win,
But like each true supporter
I'm loyal through thick and thin!'

Acknowledging his stout defence
I passed possession on
And listened to the rallying call
Of a fan of Wimbledon.

'Boys, you're so predictable!'
Was her opening, top-spin serve.
"Why don't you watch some tennis,
Witness artistry and nerve?

It's poetry in motion
When drop shots kiss the court
Yet it's a battle of the gladiators
Of the most athletic sort.'

The volley of abuse received
Put McEnroe to shame
So I looked to the athletics fan,
A disciple of THE Games.

'Now what could be more natural
Than to run, to jump, to throw?
In all our dreams we're Usain Bolt
When the starter's pistol goes.

Our heroes win gold medals,
Not laurel wreaths from Greece,
And their dedicated training
Brings fulfilment and release

From the rat race of the city
And inspires us to get fit -
So forget those balls and rackets
Just unpack your running kit!'

'But what about our indoor sports?'
Asked the plaintive snooker fan,
While the Welshman with the broken nose
Found it hard to understand

How his beloved rugby,
With its heaving ruck and maul,
Was not the choice of everyone
Whether round or short or tall.

To my lips I raised my whistle,
Time had beaten us in the end
And to choose an outright winner
Would be certain to offend
So I arranged a future rematch,
A chance to right more wrongs,
And if YOUR choice is different
Why don't YOU come along?

# The law of the classroom jungle

After one teenage interjection too many
He was sentenced to an hour's detention
(With no time off for good behaviour)
By a teacher who was no advocate of healthy debate.

He dragged himself from the dock
And turned to face his classmates,
Reluctant witnesses in this unfortunate case.
Much as he would have liked
To appeal this heartless verdict,
And argue the case for clemency
By appealing eloquently to the gallery,
It made sense to (ac)quit
While the going was good
And return home on parole.

And anyway, soon he would be the one
Sitting in judgement on the bench.
But this one would be opposite the teacher's house -
And it would be growing conveniently dark...

# A cross stick

A formidable lady who ran a tight ship

C ecilia Blunt had hairs on her lip
R uler in hand, she conducted our class
O pening minds just like opening jars
S evere in her manner, severe in her dress
S caring some charges, I have to confess

S oaring somehow to the challenges set
T he lessons I learned, they stay with me yet
I was inspired, I fell under her spell
C ollege soon beckoned, job prospects as well
K ey to it all, a pace set so well.

# Come on in, the plot is lovely!

To open a book is to stand at the edge
Of an ocean of words that surge and sway
With a mind of their own. The currents are deep
But adventure awaits and you'll remember the day
You first dived in the text, in the foaming print
And the words swept past in a bubbling rush
Sucking you down to the story's depths
Where the villains schemed and the damsels gushed.

What treasures you glimpsed at each chapter's end
And where might your imagination lead?
How scared you were as your air ran short
Yet still consumed by the need to read
You shot to the surface to fill your lungs
Then dived once more to the writer's reef
Where the jagged spines of awaiting books
Held a fascination beyond belief.

# The cat's whiskers (after T.S. Eliot)

Macavity's a Mystery Cat: he's called the
Hidden Paw -

For he's the pupil criminal who can defy the law.

He's the bafflement of Scotland Yard, he's
every school's despair:

For when they reach the scene of crime -
Macavity's not there.


And when a teacher's looking round, her coffee
cup to find,

Or the photocopier's playing up and it
seems it's lost its mind,

When the minibus is obstinate and won't
agree to start,

Or a swimming bag goes missing and you
simply must depart,

Or the secretary's laptop's down and she's
pulling out her hair:

Ay, there's the wonder of the thing! Macavity's not
there!

Macavity, Macavity, there's no one like Macavity,

He's broken every playground rule, he breaks the
laws of gravity.

His powers of levitation may take him to the roof,

But down the fire escape he strolls, so cool
and so aloof!

You may seek him in the Games shed,
you may seek him in the loo,

And when you think he's in Year One, he's
really in Year Two!


Macavity's a clever one, he's very tall and thin,

Yet he never seems to manage quite to hand his
homework in.

He leans his chair to tipping point, he fiddles
with his pens,

He'll manipulate the classroom clock to make
the lesson end.

He'll open doors for passing staff, then imitate
their walk,

He thinks that 'working quietly' means he's
allowed to talk!

Macavity's a Mystery Cat, he's called the
Hidden Paw -

For he's the pupil criminal who can defy school law.

He's the bafflement of teaching staff, the
SMT's despair,

For when they reach the scene of crime,
Macavity's not there!


He always has an alibi, with one or two to spare,

For adults it is difficult to ever find his lair.

When the Head of Maths discovers that his
whiteboard's on the blink,

Or the kitchen staff find sausages all
swimming in their sink,

Whatever time the crime took place,
Macavity has left,

With those who hold authority frustrated and bereft.


But while this fiend in feline shape is the
envy of his peers,

The Head will surely be avenged - although it
may take years!

# With friends like these...

Playground secrets spread like butter
Glisten on each teller's lips
And with each new poisoned morsel
The mask of so called friendship slips.

They may be young, these break time actors,
But words strike home with deadly aim
As barbs of jealous rumour, gossip
Dig into their victim's name.

She, meanwhile, is blithely skipping,
The rope a whirling, whizzing blur,
And when she smiles across the playground
They wave - as if they all like her.

# Grammar school sports day

On your punctuation marks,
Get ready, set... and GO!
Spectators crane their straining necks
And cheer the runners so.
My money's on the hyphen -
Across the turf he'll dash,
For the comma's bound to stop, and pause
(Or with the brackets clash).
Should I support the question mark?
There's some doubt he will compete,
And as for the ellipsis...
Well, he may not quite complete.
The finish line is now in sight,
All is strain and perspiration
As the first to breast the tape, of course,
Is the mark that's EXCLAMATION!

Across in the ampersand pit
The competition's tense
For the verb's in front at present
In the opening field event;
As for the adjective's attempts
There are no words to describe
The sequence of his 'no jumps'
As to ash his dreams subside.

Still, he will be in the relay
Where the adverb quickly runs
To hand on to the preposition
And the conjunction's having fun
Because to link is what he's born for
So the result is not in doubt,
The parts of speech will win by miles
As interjections shout!

# A contemporary witches' spell

Round about the cauldron go
In the present's entrails throw

Exhaust fumes from a four-wheel drive
Bribes that make corruption thrive
Smashed-up bottles in the gutter
Insults that the hoodies mutter
Junk food from a burger van
Sweeteners in a fizzing can
Vomit from a drunken youth
Saliva from a Pit Bull's tooth
Dripping bile from trolls on line
Lurking threat from old landmines
Poison from a tabloid sting
Interest rates that loan sharks bring
And laden boats where migrants cling

Double double toil and trouble
Fire burn and cauldron bubble
Cool it with an MP'S blood
Then the charm is firm and good.

# Power trip

I took something to school last week
To see what it might do -
And when you hear what then transpired
You may be tempted too!

For straight away life was transformed,
The course of lessons changed,
My thumb became a tyrant
And time was rearranged.

What magical device was this
For which you'd sell your soul?
You'll find it on the sofa now,
It's your remote control!

Oh my, what power it gave me
On this auspicious day,
This pupil's prayers were answered
In a MOST rewarding way!

If Maths became quite boring
I'd fast forward for a while,
The way the teacher twitched and jerked
Would really make me smile!

When Madame Jones was spouting French,
My understanding weak,
Subtitles proved a godsend -
Translations I could seek.

Then when it came to playtime
And the pleasures that we find,
Before the teacher rang the bell
I'd simply press rewind!

When Mr Brown would rant and rave,
An ogre in a suit,
I'd stand and smile so sweetly
My finger on the mute!

But all too soon my day was ended,
My wizardry in doubt;
Make sure YOU take some spares along
For batteries run out!!

# Playing Cupid

Miss Smith, our Year 5 teacher,
Is cute and calm and kind,
But as yet she has no boyfriend,
No date or Valentine.

Perhaps she needs to 'find her voice'
Or 'her confidence is weak',
For she used such words on my report
Then helped me week by week.

So now I'll try to pay her back,
To be HER guiding hand,
And on her desk I'll leave a card
To make her understand

That a colleague longs to date her,
For she brightens up his day,
His heart just skips a beat each time
She shyly looks his way.

And who could this admirer be,
The man who lies in store?
My friends and I just know he's right -
He taught us in Year 4!

# I'll seek it here, I'll seek it there...

I've given up hunting similes,
We all know what they're like,
But as fast as a speeding bullet
Or a lightning strike
I'll search for more elusive prey,
One with a profile low,
Incognito, in disguise,
It taunts a reader so.
It lurks among the lines I read
And a challenge lies in store
To capture the comparison
Dressed up as metaphor!
My eyes will be my hunting dogs,
My brain will cast its net,
To my linguistic menagerie
We'll add an inmate yet!

# Remembrance

Is a minute's silence too much to ask
Amid our daily classroom tasks?
This year and every dank November
Our soldiers' sacrifice we SHOULD remember.
Not just Tommies under constant fire,
Besieged by mud and cruel barbed wire,
But those who give their lives today
In desert sand so far away.
Such soldiers die to keep us free
So we'll pay our tributes silently
When at eleven we hear the bell -
And remember those who fought so well.

# Say it with flowers (after R. McGough)

To remember the dead with our poppies
You might think in this age to be soppy
But a corpse on barbed wire that lies floppy
Or has drowned in foul mud that is sloppy
Shows slaughter we never should copy
Lives given we honour... with poppies.

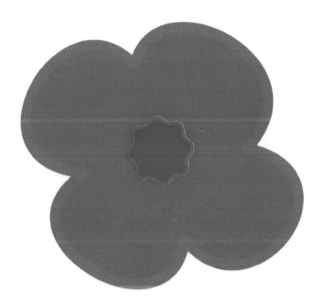

## Lest We Forget.

# Subject to my affection...

My life has changed since she arrived
As now I pay attention
In daily lessons without fail
For she's subject to my affection.
Our History may be somewhat short
But she's Poetry in motion
When she's on the Netball court
And I sometimes have a notion
While I study her Geography
That one day the height of bliss
Would be to prove our Chemistry
In the sharing of a kiss.
Dark of hair with flashing eyes
She could be my Latin lover,
In Maths I'd write her number
Inside my textbook cover.
Her voice is Music to my ears,
In English she casts a spell,
She makes an Art of project work
And if things turn out well
I'll have more progress to report
And I'll really make the grade -
For she's subject to my affection
Putting others in the shade!

# Marble

Admire my smooth strength
And imagine being prised from Italian hillsides
Then heaved on board sailing ships
Bound for the markets of Europe

Listen to traders haggling over me
Eager to impress their customers
Who will then employ
Only the finest craftsmen
To manipulate my cool contours

Prized by the Archers' Guild
As an advertisement for power
See me in this still life painting
Bearing the trappings of wealth
On my smooth shoulders.

# Just imagine

The sun is the tallest sunflower
Shedding warming petals
The moon is a silver button
On a pupil's blazer
The sun is a ripe orange
So juicy and so tempting
The moon is a flickering candle
Lighting up your darkness
The sun is a freshly-baked biscuit
Resting on a bright blue tray
The moon is a pale grey eyeball
Watching your every move
The sun is a yellow football
Kicked high into the heavens
The moon is a sparkling DVD
Featuring the brightest stars
It is also the mouth
Of a cool grey cave
Inviting you in...

HOLIDAYS

# Speedy boarding

Planning an escape to the Continent
I laboured under the misapprehension
That I would be saving time
That the shortest distance between two points
Would be a straight (air) line

But I queued for the car park at the dawn of the day
I queued for the check-in when I entered the fray
I queued for security where my bag was x-rayed
I queued then for boarding as the end game was played.

Sinking at last into my seat by the aisle
I was forced to recalibrate my expectations
Realisation dawning that I had left home
almost four hours ago
But had yet to leave this green and pleasant land.

Icarus-like, I had tried it for size
A bid in good faith to take to the skies
But blood pressure alone was now on the rise
And, unlike the plane, it was time that just flies...

# Mad March hair

The wind is an unruly child today:
He delights in pestering me,
In tugging impatiently at my clothing
And snatching paper bags from my shopper's grasp.

Eventually, as if taking umbrage at being ignored,
He sends my flat cap spinning through the air
like a tweed frisbee.
He then whoops with delight at the result,
The tattered bird's nest on my head.

# Seaside ice cream

A cold kiss on a hot day
That crisp cone still holds sway
Sticky smears on a child's face
Fat sun sinks at a snail's pace
Castle turrets crumbling now
Sand licked clean by each wave's prow.

# A performance to die for

Taking her cue from a midnight sky

She glides into the theatre of our garden.

Hers may only be a walk on part, a deadly cameo,

But that assassin grin will linger like the
Cheshire Cat's

And that unforgettable rankness will taint the air

Long after she has taken her curtain call,

Her time in the spotlight moon complete.

# Mall fever (after John Masefield)

I must go down to the mall again, to the
only place I'm free,

And all I ask is my mobile phone to take the
next selfie,

And a friend's laugh and fast food and the
news that's breaking,

And a shared grin at a text sent and some
mischief making.

I must go down to the mall again, for the
train on the Central Line

Is an old train and a slow train that's busy
all the time;

And all I ask is the next sale where designer
labels beckon,

And a black dress or a handbag which I'll pay
for within seconds.

I must go down to the mall again, to the
vagrant shopper's life,

To the crowd's way and the youth's way, free
from parental strife;

And all I ask is a coffee cup and a
giggling fellow buyer,

And a full bag on my train seat and a
credit limit higher.

# Time and tide

Storm clouds slide from view
And the sea breathes its secrets
With long and heartfelt sighs.
Marbled water reaches out
With white insistent fingers
To claw at moistened pebbles
But these salty caresses are spurned
As the shore, once again,
Turns coldly away.

# Positano

A typical Italian exercise
In style over substance,
This hillside house of cards
Threatens languidly to topple
Into the soft Mediterranean below.

Yet the sheer bravura, the defiance
Of this delicate balancing act,
Makes my spirits rise -
Like bubbles in a crisp Prosecco.

# Holiday haikus

Days stretch endlessly
Plump with possibilities
Homework's yoke shrugged off

Yet like elastic
Time will snatch this freedom back
As summer speeds past

Flickering montage
Featuring balmy evenings
And idle chatter

Until, merciless
In its awful certainty,
Autumn term arrives

# All that jazz

The pianist's pale fingers
Scatter notes which hang
In the air and then dissolve
Into the urgent rhythm you provide.

Your hands span the strings
Of your cradled bass
As they tug and they glide

Then slide to finesse
A resonance so eloquent
That it stills the murmur of conversation
With its taut, insistent tones.

The only other movement
Is the gliding dance of waiters
Drawn to the firefly glow
Of diners' table lamps.

# Autumn alchemy

It is the perfect late September day.

A low gold sun in a stonewashed denim sky

Burnishes the empty urgencies of the suburbs

While squirrels forage tirelessly, each
acorn excavation

Insurance against the deprivations of a
harsher winter.

At the lawn's edge leaves crunch under my feet

Like crumpled crisp packets on the nearby
pavement.

Meanwhile, somewhere on the blue horizon,

A jet's roar drains imperceptibly away

Like the flashbulb brilliance of this perfect day...

# Conkers

After a stormy night
I pick my way across
The damp autumn grass
Strewn with barbed confetti.
Each conker bristles with possibilities -
One might be a knight's mace
Swung weightily through battlefield air
Before thudding to the ground in defeat.
Another, perhaps, a sea urchin
Clinging burr-like to its wet companions
Imprisoned in a quayside creel.

Eventually I pocket one
Out of schoolboy habit
And with each homeward step
I relish its familiar prickle
Against a now older thigh.

# Bonfire Night, 1917

Each sniper's sly shot was his banger
Each whistling artillery shell his rocket
Crackling machine guns were his jumping jacks
Seeping, gushing gas shells his Roman candles
The stuttering rifle he held was his sparkler
And each shell shocked flailing of arms and legs
His own hellish Catherine wheel.

# Burns Night toast

His verse is like the finest dram
That's drunk on Hogmanay
His words in the vernacular
Still speak to us today

As rich as all his lyric gifts
Was the landscape of his birth
Where he grew and learned to work
The fertile Ayrshire earth

Till all the crops are gathered in
And the rocks melt with the sun
The Scots will love their Rabbie Burns
For the lassies' hearts he won

So fare thee well our Scottish bard
And we'll toast your health today
And then again in years to come
From the valley to the brae

# The greatest gift

To Bethlehem she'd journeyed, upon a donkey's back,

No special welcome beckoned, accommodation lacked

In all the places asked at, until at last they found

The barest stable waiting, where glory shone around

As the greatest gift the world had seen, the precious son of God,

Was delivered in the open where hooves of beasts had trod.


No television adverts, no streaming on the Net,

No teenage fingers texting, no flashing neon yet,

Instead, one star - and shepherds - then wise men from the east

Announced this greatest gift of all and how their eyes did feast

Upon the infant swaddled there, a present from on high,

That would change their lives forever yet in a manger lie.

No gaudy, glossy paper wrapped up this
newborn child,

He lay in shifting straw instead, adored by
Mary mild.

## Twelfth Night blues

Impatient hands are undressing me now
And I shed needle tears,
Shorn of glittering tinsel and lights
My farewell is your start of the year.

Tradition dictates that this is my fate
When the Wise Men visit the Child,
Their gifts endure for eternity
While I stand bare and defiled.

So do what you will on this Twelfth Night -
Bring an end to my Christmas story,
But at least I too have been adored
And known a fleeting glory.

PAST, PRESENT
AND FUTURE DAYS

# In the red

'Spend it wisely,' my parents might have said,

'For there'll be no more when it has gone.'

Yet like the boy who relishes the half-crown heft

Of a week's pocket money,

But is equally desperate to rid himself of it,

I proceeded to paint the town red... with Time.

Spendthrift extraordinaire, I was prodigal in my
abandon.

And sprees were my youthful speciality.


And now? Well now I would give anything,

Simply anything, to have my time over again -

The time of my life.

# Oh what a circus...

Roll up, roll up and see
The amazing hypnotised family!
Mouths agape, expressions blank,
Watch them squatting settee shaped,
United by remote control
Yet as remote as ever in their lives.
Marvel at their ability
To synchronise their forks and knives
With scarce a glance at balanced plates
Or food as easily digestible and bland
As the fare dished up by countless stations.
Gasp as they multi-task with practised hands,
Juggling phones to surf and text
As another day drains emptily away
And the curtain falls on lives more black and white
Than colour, more blank even than their eyes.

# The cyclist (after Rupert Brooke)

If I should die, think only this of me:
That there's some corner of a London street
That is for ever Lycra. There shall be
On that hard road an ugly buckled heap;
A wheel that pedals pushed, that brakes held back
Before the fates and traffic did conspire;
Symbol of freedom on both road and track,
Crushed by a lorry's brutish tyre.

# Mobiles (after William Wordsworth)

I wandered lonely as a cloud
That drifts above the traffic cones,
When all at once I saw a crowd
Of beeping, pulsing mobile phones,
Outside the office, inside the shops
Texting and calling never stops.

Continuous as the stars that shine
And sparkle in a velvet sky,
They cast a spell with each new sign,
Each symbol that distracts the eye:
A hundred saw I at a glance
Putting their victims in a trance.

# Just desserts

I'm that forgotten tin of rice pudding
Pushed to the back of the shelf
Little old ladies can't see me
In shadow I pity myself
But wait, there is a hand that is reaching
And eyes that look straight into mine
I'm gripped by the firmest of handshakes
And I know - that at last - it's my time!

# Brain salad surgery

Imagine the scene at the doctors', the chaos that might well ensue

If their doors were to be thrown open to every vegetable that queued,

Each a suitable case for treatment, presenting symptoms quite unique

From the pea with a split personality to the artichoke that would not speak;

The hot flushes of the red-faced beetroot, the anorexic celery stick,

The cress-fallen leaves left trapped in their bag, never a shopper's pick.

'Feel my pulse!' would demand each lentil, while the onion who'd lost his spring

Would be advised to spend time with some rocket and feel the boost that this would bring!

# Initial disaster

AP fell out of bed, as usual,
To land in a half-conscious heap;
Life was so much more dangerous
When awake and not safely asleep.

AP stumbled into the bathroom
Where he scalded himself in the shower,
And when he cut himself shaving
It was all in the very first hour!

AP treated the stairs with due caution
And sighed with relief at their foot,
But tripped in the lounge on the fireplace,
His reward a face full of soot.

His kitchen a minefield as ever,
Sharp edges and sockets galore,
AP settled simply for cornflakes
But then knocked his bowl on the floor.

The milk made for slippery lino,
Like a skater he glided along,
Went head first into a cupboard
Thinking, 'What else now can go wrong?'

Recovering MOST of his senses
AP made his way to the door:
Perhaps he'd be safe at the office
Even though his body felt sore.

So he picked up his coat and his briefcase,
Turned the handle and promptly stepped out;
But the wind slammed the door in an instant,
He let out an agonised shout.

All his keys had been left on the table,
He was locked out of both house and car;
He then felt the first falling raindrop,
Heard the rumble of thunder afar.

He knew that the gods were against him -
Even the battery was flat in his phone -
He was doomed to be dogged by disaster
Because he was Accident Prone!

So remember in times that are taxing,
Or when Fate cuts you off at the knees,
It's never as bad as it might be
For your initials are not A and P!

# Into orbit

Ten... nine... eight
I can hardly wait
Seven... six... five
I'm feeling so alive
Four... three... two
No checking left to do
I'm pointing at the sun
And I'm blasting off on... one!

I'm drifting through deep space
In slow motion past the stars
While down below you race
Impatient in your cars.
The beauty of our world
Now takes my breath away
New glories are unfurled
Beneath me night and day.

# A cautionary tale (after H. Belloc)

You know, at least you ought to know,
For I have often told you so,
That mobile phones will cause you grief
And that each call, however brief,
Can interrupt a presentation,
Can pinpoint you in your location,
Can beep and flash and catch your eye,
Can make your boss in anguish cry.
So please pay heed to Mark's downfall
And resist your handheld siren's call.
For on one inauspicious day,
A vital contract came his way
Which merited his full attention
On small print issues he would mention
In a later, vital meeting
When with smiles the client greeting
He would dot the Is and cross the Ts,
Putting colleagues at their ease,
Ensuring millions came their way
And at the top their firm would stay.
But as he scanned a complex clause
An ill-timed text forced him to pause,
His detailed train of thought derailed
By a running joke and what was entailed,
And so key facts were overlooked -

His firm's financial goose was cooked -
Which meant that Mark must pay the price,
That in his veins his blood was ice.
His career flashed past before his eyes
Dismissal came as no surprise.
Let Mark's demise speak to us all...
Let us ignore incoming calls!

# The descent of man

A new tribe walks among us
Whose eyes look always down;
They do not see what we see,
The wondrous world around,
Instead their sight is shackled,
A phone their ball and chain,
And how I long to free them,
To make them whole again.
Their ears too are imprisoned,
By headphones' blacksmith beat,
So that they miss life's music
And the rhythm of the street;
Instead they trudge the pavements
With scarce an upward glance,
No longer bold young dreamers,
Just victims in a trance.

# A slippery slope

How easy it seemed to tell that first lie,
To be economical with the truth,
To select the line of least resistance.
Then, having broken the ice, so to speak,
I tried deception, artistic licence
And other soft brands in the falsehoods range.

Before I knew it, I was spinning yarns
Then experimenting by crying wolf,
Telling porkies and pulling a fast one.
Mainlining soon in my downward spiral
I proceeded from lying through my teeth
To darker corners of mendacity,
Pushing the envelope with glib relish.

Of course, I promise to one day give up -
But who can believe a word that I say?

# Song cycle

Once upon a musical time
She gave birth to a song
And not just any song...

The words came first,
Spilling onto the page
In a hot liquid rush,
Before she picked up her guitar
And plucked patiently at the strings
As if panning for gold.

Forehead furrowed
She mouthed the chorus
Until her prayers were answered
And time stood still,
The notes falling into perfect place
In an act of musical alchemy.

But when she sold her song
The spell was somehow broken
As it was fashioned by others,
Shaped and polished to a studio sparkle,
Split into session players' parts
And forcibly restrained
In a commercial straitjacket.

And now? Well now her song
Has been adopted by the world.
She hears it clamouring
For attention on the radio,
Leaking from speakers in lifts,
Buzzing in a hundred headphones
And even listens to its plastic voice
When she is put on hold.

Once upon a musical time
She gave birth to this song
But now it just breaks her heart.

# The Titanic

In 1912 Southampton Docks
Were filled with cheering crowds,
The drums were banged and flags were waved,
The sky seemed free from clouds.
This colossal ship was Queen of the Water -
Yet trouble would come from an icy quarter.

Off they sailed on that April day
On an unsinkable ship with hearts so gay;
The maiden voyage was a great event,
In keeping with the fortunes spent,
The rich and famous dressed in style
And every face still bore a smile.

On the bridge the crew were calm,
Convinced that naught could do them harm,
While people danced, musicians played
And silver knives and forks were laid;
Shimmering through the night they sped
And no one thought of rest or bed.
Titanic crossed vast oceans deep
With more than half the world asleep,
A fairytale vessel ablaze with light
That soon would feel the iceberg's bite...

It tore the hull with jagged teeth,
The damage done defied belief;
Metal buckled, water gushed,
Along the corridors it rushed,
A giant brought down to its knees
Titanic staggered - in icy seas.
To lifeboat stations people fled
Where yet more anguish lay ahead,
The rich and powerful took their places
But there lacked sufficient spaces:
The steerage class beneath the deck
Would surely perish with the wreck.

Through heaving masses husbands fought,
Each face a desperate mask,
To find a berth for wife and child
The all-consuming task.
As minutes passed, the sea's caress
Like poison numbed the soul
Of each poor wretch still left aboard
This night as black as coal.
They could but watch the lifeboats leave
And wonder at their fate,
For an icy headstone would mark their grave
While the world would mark the date
When Nature played an April Fool

On the arrogance of Man,
Who thought he'd tamed the ocean's might
With his metal master plan.

For the 'Unsinkable' sank in a few short hours
And black the headlines bloomed, like flowers.

# By my side

I opened the cupboard door
To find your collar and your lead
Hanging limply from a hook
And I remembered
The thousand bendings-down
To attach one to the other
While you wriggled in anticipation,
Your tail thumping its tattoo
Against my thigh.

And then I saw your bowls
Stacked sadly in the corner
And I remembered their metallic ring
As you butted them against the skirting board
With your domed head
And your questing, glistening snout.
And then, as I shut the cupboard door,

The sudden waft of air
Brought back your earthy scent
And you were by my side again.
And I knew that this day would be richer,
Simply by being shared.

WRITING WAYS

## SCHOOLDAYS

1. Flight of Fancy - Although not a 'rhyming poem', what structural patterns can you find in terms of alliteration and assonance? Could you write a poem about the opportunities a new year provides? You could have some fun with plays on words involving 'resolution/blank piece of paper/new leaf...'

2. Tree in the Playground - Is there an object or a particular spot in your home or school which you could give a voice to? (Clock/Gates/TV...?) Using personification can lead to a powerful, fresh perspective.

3. The Great Debate - Could you add a verse or two to this poem in support of your favourite sport or game? Aim to maintain the rhyme scheme and choose fairly simple words to end lines 2 and 4 of each verse in order to make your job easier. Challenge friends to do the same.

4. The Law of the Classroom Jungle - This poem uses all sorts of legal terms as its framework. Could you write about classroom life using language connected to another profession such as

the Army/Medicine/Sport/Building? This poem has a dark undertone and is written from the pupil's point of view. What might the teacher have written about the same incident, however?

5. A Cross Stick - Forgive the pun in the title! Acrostics have always been popular so try one of your own - it doesn't have to rhyme.

   Discuss what it is that makes Miss Blunt a 'good' teacher.

6. Come on in, the plot is lovely - Here nautical imagery has been used to capture the joy of reading. Could you add a line or two using a similar approach, or even sum up the pleasure a good book offers using terms linked to food/travel/holidays?

7. The Cat's Whiskers - If you are not familiar with the original, do have a look at T.S. Eliot's famous poem in 'Old Possum's Book of Practical Cats'. Then try to imagine the havoc Macavity might wreak in your school or home! Can you write your own verses using a similar rhyme scheme? Writing parodies helps you to appreciate the patterns involved.

8.  With friends like these... We are not always as kind as we should be to our 'friends'. Try using this poem or William Blake's ' A Poison Tree' as a spur to PSHE discussion. Could you write a more positive poem about being a true friend?

9.  Grammar School Sports Day - Ask a teacher or classmate to read this aloud. See who can spot the exact number of parts of speech that are mentioned. Can you think of any other athletic puns that might have been included?

10. A Contemporary Witches' Spell - Shakespeare never goes out of fashion and never fails to make us think. Could you add your own ingredients to this spell to say something about 21st Century life? Aim to use the rhyming couplets pattern.

11. Power Trip - Every pupil's dream come true! But what would you do with YOUR remote control? Try to add a verse or two of your own, aiming where possible to end lines 2/4 with relatively simple words offering a wide range of rhymes.

12. Playing Cupid - Could you write an amusing Valentine's Day poem using some typical phrases from YOUR school report?

13. I'll seek it here, I'll seek it there... Can you identify the similes and metaphors which provide the framework for this poem? Could you extend it by 'hunting' another figure of speech, such as hyperbole or onomatopoeia?

14. Remembrance/Say it with Flowers - Here are two
15  contrasting approaches to writing about wartime sacrifice. How could you vary things? Try a shape poem, for example, using a poppy or cross or a Shakespeare parody beginning 'To fight or not to fight'...

16. Subject to my Affection - Try making a list of the subjects mentioned here and any others you can think of. What other phrases in our language can you think of that include these names? Pick one to begin your poem and see where your imagination takes you!

17. Marble - This poem came out of the National Gallery's 'Take One Picture' scheme. 'Still Life with Drinking Horn' was the painting in question, but you could look closely at any work of art and try personifying a particular object or feature.

18. Just Imagine - This list poem uses metaphorical
    ideas generated in class. Could you extend the
    list or write your own version? Alternatively,
    substitute the sun and moon for other objects.

## HOLIDAYS

19. Speedy Boarding - Travel invariably involves
    frustration! How would you write about traffic
    jams/delays on the underground/train
    cancellations etc?

20. Mad March Hair - Which type of weather could
    you personify? Rain/thunder/snow? Some of the
    ideas you generate could also be used to 'lift' your
    creative writing.

21. A performance to die for - Try reading this to a
    friend. Can they identify the animal being
    described? Could you think of other ways to
    capture the essential nature of a fox? Are there
    other theatrical terms which you could include?

22. Mall Fever - Have a look at 'Sea Fever' by John
    Masefield and compare it with this parody. Does
    it help you to understand how the rhyme scheme
    works? Could you add your own verse about
    shopping?

23. Seaside Ice Cream - Sometimes a short, simple poem is all you need to capture the essence of a place or a moment in time. Could you add other rhyming couplets which sum up a day at the seaside?

24. Time and Tide - You might consider the effect of the long vowel sounds in this poem. Could you personify the sea in your own verse? Don't try to rhyme, just immerse yourself in the sound and rhythm of your words.

25. Positano - Is there any significance to the layout of this poem? How would you sum up a favourite place in ten lines or less?

26. Holiday Haikus - Working to the classic pattern of 5/7/5 syllables, how might you sum up aspects of the school holidays? As the Haiku form captures a moment in time perfectly, perhaps you could keep a diary and write one for each day.

27. All that Jazz - This was written after watching my son play at Ronnie Scott's, the famous London jazz venue. Without trying to rhyme, how would you sum up the sound and character of a particular instrument?

28. Autumn Alchemy - Although not a rhyming poem, assonance helps to provide a framework for the ideas that feature. What examples can you find?

29. Conkers - Here autumn is approached in a different way. Develop your own use of senses by holding and examining some conkers. Make a note of any ideas that come to you, however odd they first appear, then try combining them in different ways until a poem emerges.

30. Bonfire Night 1917 - Fireworks provide a rich source of imagery and ideas and here they help to shed light on the First World War. How would you use fireworks terminology to write about another topic such as behaviour or weather?

31. Burns Night Toast - If you don't know much about the life and times of Robert Burns, do a little digging. As we mark the 400th anniversary of Shakespeare's death, how would you celebrate his life in a similar way?

32. The Greatest Gift - In increasingly commercial times, the true meaning of Christmas sometimes disappears. How could you write about the best present of all? You could experiment with an acrostic, a shape poem or your own carol.

33. Twelfth Night Blues - A Christmas tree's poignant story. But what would YOUR tree say if you gave it a voice? Imagine, perhaps, that it has watched your family closely during the highs and lows of the festive season...

## PAST, PRESENT AND FUTURE DAYS

34. In the Red - It is so easy to waste time and then regret it! Here, money has been used as a connecting theme but is there another you could use such as food and drink, or the environment?

35. Oh What a Circus... Television isn't necessarily a bad thing, of course, so could you write a poem in its defence using more circus or performance terminology?

36. The Cyclist - This is a topical issue. Is there another famous poem you could parody to make further points about the pros and cons of cycling?

37. Mobiles - See 36 above.

38. Just Desserts - As a further exercise in personification, pick an everyday object from your home or school and imagine how it might be feeling.

39. Brain Salad Surgery - There are lots of puns or plays on words here. Can you think of any others for different vegetables? Could you write a similar fruit salad response?

40. Initial Disaster - Try reading this to a friend or family member. Can they guess what A and P stand for before the end of the poem? Try adding other verses in which everything seems to go wrong. Or try a school version using your own experience.

41. Into Orbit - How do the vowel sounds affect the mood in the second half of this simple poem? Imagine that you were drifting in space; how could you use your senses to capture such an experience?

42. A Cautionary Tale - Have a look at 'Jim' by Hilaire Belloc and count the syllables in each line. Once you are familiar with the rhythm, try writing lines about a pupil who disobeys the rules at school. What might the consequences be?

43. The Descent of Man - You will probably feel very differently about technology. Write a response which outlines its plus points.

44. A Slippery Slope - This is an example of a sonnet, though you can be flexible with the rhyme scheme in your fourteen lines. Think about how it feels to tell a lie and see if you can add a few lines containing other variations on the theme.

45. Song Cycle - Who else might create something which is then possessed by others? A painter/author/tailor? Try to express how such a person might feel in a similar situation.

46. The Titanic - This narrative poem was written for a group performance. Can you think of another famous event that could be recreated in such a way? Moon Landing? The Battle of Hastings? How would your class then act out the resulting poem?

47. By My Side - Is there an evocative object at home that reminds you of a person or animal? Aim to use your senses to capture the depth of your emotion.